# EGGS
## *in Your* NEST

# EGGS
## *in Your* NEST

A proven, prudent plan that **you can do** to put lots
of eggs in your retirement basket.

Owen Little

## müllerhaus
### [LEGACY]

TULSA

**Eggs in Your Nest**
Written by Owen Little

ISBN-13: 978-0-9978410-7-7
Library of Congress Control Number: 2018958397

Published in the United States by Müllerhaus Publishing Arts, Inc.
DBA Müllerhaus Legacy
5200 South Yale Ave, Penthouse | Tulsa, Oklahoma 74135
www.MullerhausLegacy.com

Cover and Interior Design by Laura Hyde | Müllerhaus Legacy

# DEDICATION

In memory of our father, who prepared my
younger brother and me very well for lifetime
financial responsibilities. We regret this book
was not written in time for him to have seen it.

# CONTENTS

# FOREWORD

Throughout the last 50 years of the 20th century, the prudent, easiest, and most cost-effective way to self-manage a retirement savings stock/bond equities market portfolio was to depend on low-fee index funds.

As you'll see in Appendix's S&P 500 history, the 90s were its best decade, with 16.11% average annual returns and a decade return of 315.75%. The 70s were the most discouraging decade, with only 3.2% in average annual returns and a decade return of 17.25%. Long-term 50 year annual average return was 10.56%.

Per the oft-quoted 7 year rule, a 10% return every year for 7 years will double an investment portfolio's value. A portfolio returning 10% would therefore double 7 times in 50 years. If invested with discipline in an income tax free IRA, an initial investment of $5,000 will have become a well over half million dollar retirement fund in those 20th century years. No way, of course, that a portfolio would provide a consistent 10% return every year. But an annual average of 10% over 7 years will come close to doubling its value.

**But in the 21st century it hasn't been as easy to do as it was in the 20th, caused in the first decade because of losses, and most recently because of volatility.**

In its first decade, the S&P 500 experienced four minus years, and 2 more years that returned less than 4%. With not enough good years to provide a positive annual average, for the first time in 60 years the 2000–2009 decade had a minus annual average: -.61%. The decade return was a startling -24.10%.

How disappointing index funds would have been after these 12 years:

Bush–Gore election date, November 7, 2000:
**S&P 500 was 1431.87.**
Obama–Romney election date, November 6, 2012:
**S&P 500 was 1428.39.**

**Wow! What's our investment plan in this risky century!?! The aim of this book is to offer a proven plan to answer that question. Let's get started!**

# INTRODUCTION

*You don't need to be an expert in order to achieve satisfactory investment returns. But if you aren't, you must recognize your limitations and follow a course certain to work reasonably well. Keep things simple and don't swing for the fences...*

—WARREN BUFFETT
in his 2014 letter to
Berkshire Hathaway shareholders

What follows in this introduction are brief answers to questions you may have about my intent in writing this book.

- Who do I hope to reach?
- Why do I want to share a reasoned plan that has been tested for years and been found to reliably work well?
- Who am I to offer investment expertise to persons I do not know?

In addition, I have included occasional notes on things to look for in the plan.

## *What is the intent of this little how-to book?*

Simply put, it is to share expertise in creating and maintaining a retirement investment account acquired the old-fashioned way: by having succeeded in learning how to do that well after many years of trial and error (most reliably the latter), and by growing old enough to appreciate having the resulting assets in my senior years.

**NOTE:** *What is also appreciated is that investment assets, and the investment acumen they develop, are the most controllable retirement assets one can have.*

- Social Security is too hot a potato for any Congress to do away with, but it is subject to future limitation changes as pressures of rising numbers of retirees and their effect on national debt happen.
- A house that's owned debt-free is certain to be subject to rising maintenance costs and the possibility of damage or destruction by weather, natural disasters, or accidents of many kinds.
- A defined pension is subject to the financial health of the company that promised it, and could be reduced or even eliminated.

## *Who does this little book hope to help?*

My brief personal bio, included on page xv, may mislead one to think there's a clue in it that the reader can use to decide if the investment plan is only for people with similar life stories. Not so!

My life story is one of stable lifetime employment, raising a family, and no formal training in investment theory or practices. The hands-on trial-and-error learning experience that produced a successful investment plan was a years-long effort requiring time and money. So, yes, sharing a do-it-yourself retirement plan with financially stressed persons who have stable income, especially those with family responsibilities, single or married, is indeed a high priority. *But who else?*

1. **Persons with limited income for whatever reason must make day-to-day spending decisions that are often between choices that are all high priorities.** Saving for a far-off future is 1 of 3 options (see page xv) difficult to consider, even by those who know it should be. I heard about that challenge many times in nineteen years of volunteer income tax preparation.

   Determination to save for the future requires a will that is strong enough to overcome the difficulties. Tax return preparation is an annual opportunity for a bonus in the form of a tax refund. Most importantly, if eligible, the earned income tax credit provides a welcome addition to that refund to low-wage persons with dependents, a credit given even if no tax is owed. Tax time is an excellent opportunity for considering a contribution to a retirement fund.

2. **Very young persons with income who do not have dependents are in a good position to start and contribute to a retirement fund.** Not likely to be considered, of course,

but the outcome will be huge if they do. If started early in adult life, note the comment on potential for a very large retirement fund in the 7 year rule mentioned in the Foreword.

## Why share hard-earned investment expertise?

The plan presented in this little book has ***built-in advantages*** well beyond fee savings over what investment advice newsletters or professional wealth managers can reasonably offer. Look for what those advantages are as you consider each of the ground rules in the following chapters.

The era in which this little book is being written is one in which private company defined pensions are almost all gone, and the 401-K plans being offered in their place require that the employee must make difficult decisions on investment of their own and company contributions from a very limited choice of mutual fund offerings.

As you saw in the Foreword, 21st century stock markets have been tougher ones in which to navigate than those of the final 50 years of the 20th century.

My 2 clear choices are: share an investment plan that works well with the many individuals and families who live with stressful financial future prospects, or take a plan with no value there with me to whatever destination you believe I go to when I leave this planet.

I believe I should do the right thing rather than the easy one. This little book intends to do that, and leave it up to the readers to decide on whether to:

1. Take charge of that stressful future themselves, with confidence that they know how to go about it,
2. Pay someone to set up and maintain a retirement account, or
3. Leave their financial future to chance.

## What is my academic and employment experience?

My academic background consists of a mid-1950s UCLA degree in Anthropology and the completion of all classroom work toward a Finance MBA at San Fernando Valley State College night school. A job transfer from California to Tulsa, Oklahoma, made it too difficult to even begin to work with a far-away mentor on a thesis requirement to obtain the degree.

The employer that offered that promotion move was North American Aviation, and the reason for my and many other transfers from their California and Columbus, Ohio, plants was a big 1960s buildup in Tulsa to support the moon landing program. Because we found Tulsa to be an ideal community in which to raise a family, our family turned down later move offers and stayed in Tulsa until and beyond my retirement from that company in 1988.

## How does that justify a claim to having credibility on investment expertise?

Although I was fortunate enough to have been born into a work era when defined pensions were the norm in large corporations, being more fully prepared for the many potentially disastrous possibilities that might occur in future years was a challenge too important to ignore.

The most attractive option appeared to be investments. If you had a plan "certain to work reasonably well" that will "keep things simple," and not "swing for the fences," to borrow Mr. Buffett's recent words on the subject, and if you invested according to plan, in good years and bad, why would it not be expected to work for you and others as well as it has for me?

**If you see yourself reflected in any of the above questions and answers, including lack of financial acumen, you're a person, family, or organization I hope to reach!**

— Owen Little, June 2018

# CHAPTER ONE

# THE PLAN

*My dad once said to me, a fool with a plan can beat a genius with no plan.*

— T. BOONE PICKENS,
letter to the *New York Times*, August 3, 2009

The words most applicable to the title of this chapter in Webster's *New World College Dictionary* definition of the noun *plan* are: **"any detailed method, formulated beforehand, for doing or making something."**

Key words are "formulated beforehand". That implies that there are clear goals, that the planner understands the difficulties in meeting those goals, and that the planner has thoughtfully reasoned out a plan to overcome those difficulties.

## THE PLAN'S GOALS ARE:

1. **Create** a self-managed retirement savings fund.
2. **Average** a long-term 10% annual return.

## *Who would best manage your investments?*

Your initial choice is to either select a wealth management firm to create and manage your investments or to create and manage one yourself. Major difficulty with selecting a wealth management firm is that there's often not an unbiased 3rd party offering ratings of investment returns performance.

Other difficulties are finding a reputable firm that offers long-term 10% annual average returns or will manage low-medium income individual portfolios. Minor negative is fees.

Could one hope to create and self-manage that fund him/herself? Could one hope to do it as well as or better than a professional wealth management firm?

The following chapters will discuss steps for creating a portfolio that are thoughtful, reasonable, and, most of all, doable. Experience with this plan, well-formulated beforehand and executed with discipline, suggests that, regardless of background, **you'd** *be the best person to manage your retirement savings!*

**The 2 things most important about the plan that follows are:**
That you **have a plan** _you believe to be reasonable_, and that you **intend** to _consistently, patiently, and thoughtfully use it for making investment decisions._

## *What you will find in the following chapters:*

The next 3 chapters will advise on the steps to be taken to initiate and implement the plan, in the order you would best take them. You will be:

- Given definitions of what mutual funds and Exchange Traded Funds (ETFs) are.
- Told why buy them only.
- Told what the 5 kinds of funds you can buy are.
- Told the 2 kinds of funds you will buy.
- Told the significant differences between mutual funds and ETFs.
- Told what Quality and Risk standards of the plan are, and why you need them.

The 2 chapters that follow define benchmarks, what to look for when selecting a broker—a very important contribution to future success—and provide tips on how to select funds to be purchased.

You will make bad decisions in an ever-changing market, as Warren Buffett and every other investor does. Do not let that discourage you from being disciplined in following the plan; it works.

Your ability to make increasingly better decisions will improve as your experience grows.

Chapters Five through Seven provide IRA options information and recommendations, examples of useful plan applications other than retirement accounts, explanation of how YTD percentage returns are calculated, an epilogue that summarizes the urgent need for a retirement plan that can be self-managed, and a glossary of investment terms.

# CHAPTER TWO

# WHAT TO BUY

1. *Invest only in mutual funds, including those called an Exchange Traded Fund (ETF), or in guaranteed-result equities, e.g., bank CDs or money market funds.*

**What is a mutual fund?**

A mutual fund has a fund manager, identified by name, who does selection of the stock and bond equities in it. Individual and organization investors buy shares in the mutual fund. You will be investing in that fund manager.

**Why invest in mutual funds only?**

It relieves the investor of responsibility for selecting equities with only very limited knowledge about the thousands of companies that are listed in the stock/bond markets. That's the manager's full-time job, and that person will have huge pay incentives to outperform other mutual fund managers.

It spreads your risk and diversifies your portfolio.

There is readily available third-party information on fund managers' performance that can be compared. A trusted firm that provides detailed information on fund manager performance to investors and your broker is Morningstar.

### What is the difference between mutual funds and ETFs?

Mutual fund trades are transacted at closing price in the evening of each trading day; ETFs are traded like stocks during the day at constantly changing prices.

#### Mutual Funds:
- Are bought and sold evenings only at a daily closing price.
- Cannot be bought with a broker loan called margin.
- There is seldom a commission on buys or sales.
- Minimum investment is required.

#### ETFs:
- Are traded like stocks all day at price of the moment.
- Orders can be price and stop limited, and can be traded on margin.
- Usually include a commission on buys and sales.
- No minimum investment.

**NOTE:** *You will often see reference to the phrase "no load" funds, and there are very many of them.*

"Load" is a term for a commission or fee you would have to pay your broker when you purchase or sell a mutual fund. There are several potential reasons for a fee to be required, one of which would be to discourage purchase of a fund owned by a competitor broker. There is little reason, however, for you to pay that fee, as it has nothing to do with the value of or returns history of the fund. Research has demonstrated that "load" funds' average returns are no better than those of "no load" funds.

Your aim is to put as much of your investment money to work for **you**, not your broker, so do not buy a "load" fund unless you believe you have a very compelling reason to do so.

## What kind of mutual funds can you buy?

- **Money market** funds are automatically purchased for you by your broker if you have cash in your portfolio. They earn interest, offer lowest returns and provide the lowest risk.
- **Bond** funds offer what's often called "fixed income". They have higher returns than money market funds, but also have higher risk.
- **Stock** funds select company stocks to purchase. There are alternatives available that identify specializations such as Large Cap, Mid Cap, or Small Cap describing comparative company size. Stock funds returns are greatest, but so is risk.
- **Category** funds also identify specializations such as industry or geographic region in their titles.
- **Balanced** funds hold a diverse mixture of stocks, bonds, and cash in order to minimize market risk.

## What kind of mutual funds *will* you buy?

Just 2, for the reasons given on the following pages.

You will **hire** the best Moderate Balanced fund managers in the country to provide the majority of your portfolio.

The remainder of your portfolio will be **selected** Category funds.

## 2. *From 50% to 70% of your portfolio will be invested in the best <u>Moderate Balanced funds</u> available.*

Logic for this plan requirement is that the best Moderate Balanced funds will provide around 7% to 9 % average returns long-term. Category funds will get you to the 10% average annual returns goal stated in Chapter One.

**Morningstar's definition of the "Allocation—50% to 70% Equity" category:**

> *"Moderate-allocation funds seek to provide both capital appreciation and income by investing in three major areas: stocks, bonds, and cash. These funds tend to hold larger positions in stocks than conservative-allocation funds. These funds typically have 50% to 70% of assets in equities and the remainder in fixed income and cash."*

**Reason for selecting Moderate Allocation to be so high a %:**

Every wealth management firm aims to produce prudently-invested best returns. Key to that aim is balance in a portfolio. Some are better at it than others, but as noted in Chapter One, it's not easy to do research on which firms are the best performers.

## 3. *The remainder of funds to be purchased will be selected Category funds.*

You will purchase Category funds that are intended to improve chances for portfolio returns of 10% or better. Funds that can reasonably be expected to offer annual returns of 15% to 20% are what you will seek.

You can find information on the current Categories that will improve total portfolio returns by broker firm research *and by always being aware of current events.* Research capability is easily available; the broker you select will furnish lists of the long-term best-performing funds in a selected Category.

It is imperative that Category funds be carefully watched, as current conditions can change greatly and sometimes often.

**Reasons:**

    a. You cannot realistically expect that even the best balanced funds will average a 10% return over long-term years. This step is why and how you can expect to do that in your retirement savings account.

    b. Because the Morningstar Moderate Balanced YTD is an average of funds performance in that Category, even if YTD of the portfolio is not at the +10% level, this step will assure that portfolio performance will beat the benchmark defined in Chapter Three.

## 4. *Quality and Risk Standards*

Generally eliminate mutual funds/ETFs being considered for purchase to those with Morningstar **quality ratings of 4 or 5 stars** and **risk ratings of Low or Below Average.**

**Reasons:**

    a. A standard must be set to provide a way to lessen the number of possibilities for fund purchases to only those funds most consistently providing the best returns in past years. The ratings criteria come from Morningstar, a trusted ratings source for many years. Historic returns are provided for YTD and for up to 10 past years.

**NOTE:** *Use of the word "generally" is quite intentional. If the investor feels there is credible good reason to do so, the investor always can and should consider a potential exception to either standard.*

    b. As is the case in this Chapter and Chapter Three, the Morningstar ratings are readily available at your broker's website.

### Definition Statement on Morningstar Website:

*Morningstar rates mutual funds and ETFs from 1 to 5 stars based on how well they've performed (after adjusting for risk and accounting for sales charges) in comparison to similar funds and ETFs.*

*Within each Morningstar Category, the top 10% of funds and ETFs receive 5 stars and the bottom 10% receive 1 star. Funds and ETFs are rated for up to three time periods—three-, five-, and 10-years—and these ratings are combined to produce an overall rating. Funds and ETFs with less than three years of history are not rated.*

*Ratings are objective, based entirely on a mathematical evaluation of past performance. They're a useful tool for identifying funds and ETFs worthy of further research, but shouldn't be considered buy or sell signals.*

# CHAPTER THREE

# DECISIONS TO BE MADE

The benchmark decision should be as recommended below; the broker decision is your call after consideration of the potential future needs in fund purchase decisions.

**Benchmark**

At least 50% to 70% of your portfolio must be invested in the best Moderate Balanced fund managers available. To verify that you have **hired** the best Moderate Balanced fund managers, the *average* performance must be known at all times. Morningstar can provide that information daily. See Figure 1 on page 12.

If your portfolio YTD return is beating average performance, you will know that your 10% goal will be met or exceeded because of your Category funds, and if not, you will know that you need to take action to improve your returns. This standard is often called a "benchmark," but call it what you will, it will be a major key to that **built-in advantage** mentioned in the Introduction.

Because the Morningstar YTD is an *average* of funds in that category, even if YTD of your portfolio is not at the 10%+ level, your portfolio's performance will beat your benchmark.

The most reliable portfolio benchmark to beat, therefore, is third party Morningstar YTD for Moderate Balanced fund category, "Allocation—50% to 70% Equity."

## Morningstar's definition of the "Allocation—50% to 70% Equity" category:

*"Moderate-allocation funds seek to provide both capital appreciation and income by investing in three major areas: stocks, bonds, and cash. These funds tend to hold larger positions in stocks than conservative-allocation funds. These funds typically have 50% to 70% of assets in equities and the remainder in fixed income and cash."*

## Reasons:

1. Every wealth management firm aims to produce prudently-invested best returns. Key to that aim is balance in a portfolio. Some are better at it than others, but as noted in Chapter One, it's not easy to do research on which firms are the best performers. You will **hire** the best Moderate Balanced fund managers in the country to provide the majority of your portfolio.

2. Historically the best Moderate Balanced funds will provide around 7% to 9 % average annual returns long-term. The high percentage of these funds in your portfolio is intended to put you in the best position to get to the 10% average annual returns goal stated in Chapter One.

**NOTE** *on Figure 1 that there are a total of 5 Allocation (balanced) funds, 2 of them more aggressive than the moderate one, and 2 more conservative. The alternates are marked with a > pointer.*

It is tempting at times, for age, life situation, and many other reasons, to consider another of the balanced funds that might seem to be a better personal fit. The recommendation, however, is to be in the 50% to 70% Equity *Moderate* Allocation funds for long-term good returns with minimized volatility and risk.

To quickly obtain the current report to check on whether your portfolio is getting better-than-average returns or not, copy or click on the website address below and immediately add it to favorites:

**http://news.morningstar.com/fund-category-returns/**

**NOTE:** *The acronym YTD in Figure 1 means year-to-date.*

## MORNINGSTAR BENCHMARK SOURCE

**Figure 1**: Limited Reproduction of Morningstar Source for Benchmark

### Fund Category Performance: Total Returns

*Data through 3/29/2018. Returns are simple averages. Morningstar Medalists by Category*

| Allocation Funds | YTD |
| --- | --- |
| Convertibles | 1.77 |
| Target-Date 2055 | -0.53 |
| Target-Date 2045 | -0.55 |
| Target-Date 2060+ | -0.60 |
| Target-Date 2035 | -0.62 |
| Target-Date 2050 | -0.63 |
| Target-Date 2040 | -0.67 |
| Target-Date 2010 | -0.71 |
| Target-Date 2015 | -0.75 |
| Target-Date 2025 | -0.76 |
| Target-Date 2030 | -0.76 |

| Allocation Funds | YTD |
|---|---|
| Target-Date 2020 | -0/81 |
| >Allocation—85%+ Equity | -0.93 |
| Target-Date Retirement | -0.97 |
| World Allocation | -1.05 |
| >Allocation—70% to 85% Equity | -1.14 |
| >Allocation—15% to 30% Equity | -1.15 |
| >Allocation—30% to 50% Equity | -1.21 |
| Allocation—50% to 70% Equity | -1.26 |
| Tactical Allocation | -1.47 |

**Broker Selection**

An investment portfolio of mutual funds and ETFs requires that one must have established a brokerage firm account or an account with a major mutual funds provider, preferably in an IRA. More on the IRA in Chapter Five.

To execute this plan you need to set up an account with a brokerage firm.

**Research capability is an important feature to question in selecting a brokerage firm.** When needed, you must have a way to enter your plan's quality and risk standards in the firm's research programs to get a list of funds that meet them. For that and long-term customer support reasons, firms with a local office are a big factor in making this decision. Request a personal demonstration of how easily a firm's online research provides ratings data like that in Figure 2.

Since they will be the majority of your portfolio, balanced funds research is the start point in setting up a portfolio. When making this and all future Category fund purchases, a list of the few eligible funds is an essential tool. Do not consider a brokerage firm that does not offer this capability.

**To assure the widest range of top-ranked fund/ETF choices, select a widely used, low-fee brokerage firm that provides research you find to be helpful and user-friendly.** There are a number of excellent brokerage firms, and being comfortable with that very personal decision is one key to long-term success.

**Having capability to furnish more detailed reports on each of the funds being considered is very helpful, and this is the second important feature to ask about when selecting a brokerage firm.**

Examples of other helpful features:

- Morningstar Category definition; and YTD, 1-, 3-, 5-, and 10-year fund history, as applicable, in performance and risk ratings;
- Historic comparisons to competing balanced funds;
- Major company or industry holdings or regional breakdown percentages of fund holdings.

# CHAPTER FOUR

# HOW TO BUY

Once you have carefully done the preparation outlined in the preceding chapters, you are ready to make initial and future Moderate Balanced and Category fund purchase decisions. Start with the majority, Moderate Balanced funds:

Unless you are returning to or adding to a fund you know, step 1 in making a decision will be to ask the broker you have chosen to provide a list of funds that meet the quality and risk standards stated in "What to Buy" Chapter Two.

**Figure 2**: Limited Reproduction of Actual June 2018 Morningstar 10 Year Report

| Symbol | Morningstar Category (Allocation) | 10 year Ratings | Risk Rating Overall |
|--------|-----------------------------------|-----------------|---------------------|
| ABINX | 50% to 70% Equity | Above Average | Below Average |
| TWBIX | 50% to 70% Equity | Above Average | Below Average |
| MBEAX | 50% to 70% Equity | High | Below Average |
| CBLCX | 50% to 70% Equity | Above Average | Below Average |
| HEIFX | 50% to 70% Equity | Above Average | Below Average |
| JABAX | 50% to 70% Equity | High | Below Average |

| Symbol | Morningstar Category (Allocation) | 10 year Ratings | Risk Rating Overall |
|--------|-----------------------------------|-----------------|---------------------|
| MBLAX | 50% to 70% Equity | Above Average | Low |
| AOBLX | 50% to 70% Equity | Above Average | Below Average |
| SIBAX | 50% to 70% Equity | Above Average | Below Average |
| VBINX | 50% to 70% Equity | High | Below Average |
| WWIAX | 50% to 70% Equity | Above Average | Low |
| WHGIX | 50% to 70% Equity | Above Average | Low |

In the Figure 2 June 2018 report Moderate Balanced funds example, there are 12 funds that fit the plan Quality and Risk standards.

Three to five balanced funds are practical and usual in individual IRAs. As an example of how to make comparisons that will help greatly in making purchase decisions, what follows is a comparison of the current 3 high performers in Figure 2: MBEAX, JABAX, and VBINX.

Top 2 Average Returns in their 10 year history, MBEAX and JABAX, are nearly identical. MBEAX is slightly ahead, but there's not much help from those scores.

All 3 are Below Average Risk, so no help from that important statistic.

Next step will be to ask your broker to compare the above 3 funds to competing balanced funds.

Current data in the Figure 3 illustration show that in 2018 YTD and 1-year returns, JABAX has been the best performer. Advantage JABAX.

## Fund Comparisons

**Figure 3:** Fund Comparisons Illustration—real numbers as of June 30, 2018

| Fund Name | Symbol | YTD | 1 year | 3 year | 5 year | 10 year |
|---|---|---|---|---|---|---|
| James Henderson Balanced Class T | JABAX | 3.12 | 12.68 | 8.38 | 8.98 | 8.24 |
| Chicago Equity Partners Balanced Fund Class N | MBEAX | 2.05 | 11.10 | 6.84 | 8.57 | 7.67 |
| American Funds American Balanced Fund Class F-1 | BALFX | 0.83 | 9.14 | 8.54 | 9.26 | 8.39 |
| Oakmark Equity and Income Fund Investor Class | OAKBX | -1.40 | 6.56 | 5.77 | 8.16 | 6.47 |
| Category Average | | -0.13 | 6.17 | 4.67 | 6.30 | 5.60 |

**NOTE** *that BALFX had best returns in 3-year, 5-year, and 10-year performance, but would not meet quality and risk standards in a 2018 broker report.*

Two other possibilities you might look at are Rank in Category for Annual Total Returns and Expenses, in both of which JABAX was best performer.

Another report to request from your broker: How many times were the 3 Moderate Balanced funds you are comparing rank in the top 25% in Annual Total Returns. JABAX was 5 times in YTD; the prior 5 years and MBEAX and VBINX 4 times.

Narrow win for JABAX. If there had still been no clear winner, another possibility is that you might want to request from your broker a list of major industry or regional breakdown percentages of fund holdings. As you'll see in the 2 illustrations on the next page, holdings in funds that are nearly equal in producing good returns can be very different from the holdings producing them.

There is a clear difference between JABAX and MBEAX holdings. Your personal investing attitudes about caution or aggressiveness at any given time now enter in, and they will guide your selection.

Which one would you choose on the day you're reading this Chapter?

## JABAX Top Ten Holdings

**Figure 4:** Fund Top Ten Holdings Illustration—real numbers as of June 30, 2018

| Symbol | Company Name | Industry | Percent of Assets |
|--------|--------------|----------|-------------------|
| SFT | Microsoft Corp | Information Technology | 3.67% |
| MA | MasterCard, Inc. A | Information Technology | 2.98% |
| BA | Boeing | Industrials | 2.76% |
| GOOG | Alphabet, Inc. C | Information Technology | 2.23% |
| CME | CME Group In Class A | Financials | 1.95% |
| ADBE | Adobe Systems, Inc. | Information Technology | 1.89% |
| | United States Treasury Notes | | 1.88% |
| MG | Altria Group, Inc. | Consumer Staples | 1.80% |
| AAPL | Apple, Inc. | Information Technology | 1.75% |
| LYB | Lyondel Basell Industries NV | Materials | 1.74% |

## MBEAX Top Ten Holdings

**Figure 5:** Fund top Ten Holdings Illustration—real numbers as of June 30, 2018

| Symbol | Company Name | Industry | Percent of Assets |
|--------|--------------|----------|-------------------|
| AAPL | Apple, Inc. | Information Technology | 3.67% |
| AMZN | Amazon.com, Inc. | Consumer Discretionary | 2.98% |
| MSFT | Microsoft Corp | Information Technology | 2.76% |

| Symbol | Company Name | Industry | Percent of Assets |
|---|---|---|---|
| GOOG | Alphabet, Inc. C | Information Technology | 2.23% |
| FB | Facebook, Inc. A | Information Technology | 1.95% |
| | United States Treasury Notes | | 1.89% |
| | United States Treasury Notes | | 1.80% |
| | United States Treasury Notes | | 1.75% |
| | United States Treasury Notes | | 1.74% |

To help you **select** Category funds, your broker must have capability to show top-performing Categories. Typically provided would be 1-year, 3-year, 5-year, 10-year and YTD. Figures 6 and 7 below illustrate 1-year and 10-year best Category performers at the time of this writing.

## **Top-Performing Morningstar Fund Categories** as of May 31, 2018
**Figure 6:** 1-Year Categories Performance Report

- 1-Year
- 3-Year
- 5-Year
- 10-Year
- YTD

| | |
|---|---|
| Technology | +25.93% Return |
| China Region | +24.68% Return |
| Small Growth | +24.43% Return |
| Large Growth | +19.82% Return |

## Top-Performing Morningstar Fund Categories as of May 31, 2018
**Figure 7:** 10-Year Categories Performance Report

- 1-Year
- 3-Year
- 5-Year
- 10-Year
- YTD

| | |
|---|---|
| Health | +13.09% Return |
| Technology | +11.92% Return |
| Consumer Cyclical | +11.03% Return |
| Small Growth | +9.93% Return |

Detailed reports on each of the funds being considered will always be very helpful, but sooner or later the growing experience and outlook of the decision-maker will occasionally result in reason(s) to consider a fund that does not meet standards.

A report from your brokerage firm, or anywhere else that offers credible (or hopefully *incredible*!) advice, is best supplemented by being aware of national and international news. What's happening, or, better yet, coming up, may affect the current and future prices of mutual funds and ETFs. A couple of examples:

In early 2016, all candidates in the presidential campaign then underway were mentioning doing something about healthcare issues, such as huge rises in treatment costs and lack of healthcare insurance for everyone in the U.S. For the rest of that year, that caused a collapse in prices of Health Category fund prices, a leader in returns for a decade.

**At the time of this writing in early 2018:**

1. All automobile companies are focused on developing electric vehicles.
2. Some countries have passed legislation banning the sale of fossil fuel vehicles at future dates.
3. Elon Musk soon will be completing construction of a "Gigafactory" that will be annually producing as many batteries as present-day world production.

Those facts will have a number of investment implications, including impact on price of key battery materials such as lithium or cobalt.

News will occasionally have effect on balanced funds, but can be a major factor as you **select** the Category funds in the portfolio.

**CAUTION NOTE:** *The above is an illustration to clarify the details that you might look at to make purchase decisions, not in any way a balanced fund recommendation.*

Two reasons: The facts will be different on every day, and what you elect to look at is subject to your personal and market experience.

As noted earlier, Category funds can change unexpectedly and quickly, so they must be monitored closely.

**NOTE** *how often research is mentioned in this section.*

Take care to make the broker decision called for in Chapter Three carefully and patiently. It's likely to be the most important decision you'll make as an investor.

# CHAPTER FIVE

# AN IRA

As noted in the Introduction, "What's appreciated is that investment assets, and the investment acumen that they develop, are the most controllable retirement assets one can have."

An **individual retirement account,** or IRA, is an individual retirement plan that provides tax advantages for retirement savings in the United States. An **individual retirement account** is a type of "individual retirement arrangement" as described in "IRS Publication 590, Individual Retirement Arrangements (IRAs)."

There are 2 types of IRAs, a Traditional IRA established by the Employee Retirement Income Security Act (ERISA) in 1974, and a Roth IRA, established by the Taxpayer Relief Act of 1997, and named after its primary sponsor, Senator William Roth of Delaware.

Each offers tax benefits, but they are distinctly different. Either IRA can have appeal, depending on personal situations and outlooks. Basic differences are:

**Traditional IRA**

- Traditional IRA contributions are deductible from income for the year the contribution is made, lowering that year's income tax.

- Traditional IRA withdrawals are taxable income in the year taken.
- Mandatory withdrawals are required after age 70 ½.

**Summary:** A Traditional IRA increases near term income, but taxes contributions and all earnings in the year withdrawals are made.

## Roth IRA

- Roth IRA contributions are not deductible from income when made.
- Roth IRA withdrawals are not taxable income in the year they are taken.
- The Roth IRA has no mandatory withdrawal requirements at any age.

**Summary:** A Roth IRA offers no immediate income tax benefit, but all contributions and earnings are not taxable when withdrawn.

**The tax benefits are too good to ignore, and research on further details is required. But an IRA choice is yours to make, and doing that is highly recommended.**

**NOTE:** *An IRA is a long-term investment with tax benefits and other appeals, for example,*

- Never having to include in your annual (often-enough-already-stressful!) tax return any mention of market trades done in the tax year
- No mandatory withdrawal requirements
- Tax benefits to your heirs

**However, if you work for an employer that offers to match your contributions to a 401-K plan, you get an immediate investment return equal to the match. Try to contribute as much as possible to both plans.**

# CHAPTER SIX

# MANY OTHER APPLICATIONS

*"When you come to a fork in the road, take it."*

**—YOGI BERRA**

Does experience show that the plan outlined in the preceding chapters can be successfully executed by an individual with lifetime academic and job knowledge in unrelated fields and a personal life that limits the time available?

The examples below of two very different actual applications of the plan offer no guarantee, but suggest that the answer can be a qualified yes.

The focus of this booklet has been on retirement savings because of the era we're in and the millions of middle-class Americans and working poor who are stressed about their retirement future.

Defined pensions from their employers cannot be sustained by even the most responsible private or publicly held businesses, and the 401-K plans that have replaced them require employee contributions and making difficult decisions.

Some civic pensions have reached the point of bankruptcy considerations by their leaders.

Recent estimates are that Social Security and Medicare will run out of funding sooner than had been previously predicted.

Irresponsible home ownership lending practices brought the economy to its knees, and many millions of owners lost their homes to foreclosure or abandoned them in the first decades of the 21st century.

Employers must have better-educated workers in this increasingly technical era; higher education costs have risen dramatically and so has student loan debt.

It's also obvious that there are many other stressful financial situations that could be eased if individuals, families, churches, and many other organizations had a prudent and proven savings plan that *they can control.*

Allow me to demonstrate with a couple of very different personal experiences:

**EXAMPLE 1:** Shows plan returns in a portfolio created to provide investment income to Tulsa's Community Action agency (CAP). CAP has developed what has become one of the nation's most highly regarded early childhood education programs, and investment income helps fund a buildings replacement reserve account.

Inception of the portfolio, begun with a $149,488.20 start value, was in late December 2010.

## RETURNS REPORT DECEMBER 31, 2017

**Figure 8:** Example of an Organization 7-Year Performance Report

| FUND/ETF NAMES (SYMBOLS) | MARKET VALUES |
|---|---|
| iShares Edge Minimum Volume ETF (USMV) | $40,171 |
| Janus Balanced Fund (JABAX) | $45,090 |
| Matthews Asia Fund (MAPAX) | $20,438 |

| FUND/ETF NAMES (SYMBOLS) | MARKET VALUES |
|---|---|
| Parnassus Mid Cap Fund (PARMX) | $20,890 |
| Schwab Balanced Fund (SWOBX) | $39,912 |
| American Fund Income Fund (IFAFX) | $31,633 |
| Buffalo Discovery Fund (BUFTX) | $23,520 |
| Global Lithium ETF (LIT) | $23,837 |
| Power Shares S&P 500 Min Vol (SPLV) | $35,924 |
| **Total** | **$277,415** |

### AVERAGE ANNUAL RETURNS REPORT CARD SUMMARY

| YTD | 1 YEAR | 3 YEAR | 5 YEAR | 10 YEAR | SINCE INCEPTION |
|---|---|---|---|---|---|
| | 17.89% | 5.90% | 10.70% | NA | 12.23% |

Figure 8 is a limited copy from an annually audited CAP Finance Department report to the organization owning the portfolio.

Compared to 4 major wealth management groups in the author's residential city, the plan ground rules' **built-in advantages** mentioned in the Introduction (*did you find them?*) provided #1 results in 5 of the 7 years between 2011 and 2017. The other 2 years, 2012 and 2016, the same wealth management team was #1.

**Example 2:** A broker custodial portfolio begun at age 1 in 2001, is illustrated in Figure 9 below.

### RETURNS REPORT DECEMBER 31, 2004–2017

**Figure 9:** Author-Prepared Actual Grandson Custodial Portfolio Performance Summary

**Account start: 8/9/2001 (age 1)**

| | |
|---|---|
| **Purchase:** 6% zero coupon bond | **2001 Purchase price:** $3,014.81 |
| **Value at maturity in 2018:** $9,000 | **Initial mutual fund buy:** $4,020.02 |

| Returns Custodial Portfolio | S&P 500 | Date | Market Value |
|---|---|---|---|
| | | 12/31/2003 | $8,886.42 |
| 11.39% | 9.0% | 12/31/2004 | $9,898.54 |
| 7.82% | 3.0% | 12/31/2005 | $10,672.72 |
| 6.93% | 13.6% | 12/31/2006 | $11,412.52 |
| 11.16% | 3.5% | 12/31/2007` | $12,686.52 |
| (3.25%) | (35.6%) | 12/31/2008 | $12,273.67 |
| 8.86% | 23.5% | 12/31/2009 | $13,361.33 |
| 11.96% | 12.8% | 12/51/2010 | $14,959.88 |
| 2.49% | 0.0% | 12/31/2011 | $15,331.75 |
| 9.97% | 13.4% | 12/31/2012 | $16,859.63 |
| 11.63% | 29.6% | 12/31/2013 | $18,820.81 |
| 5.56% | 11.4% | 12/31/2014 | $19,868.17 |
| (.8%) | (1.2%) | 12/31/2015 | $19,883.52 |
| 3.02% | 9.5% | 12/31/2016 | $20,483.33 |
| 9.95% | 19.4% | 12/31/2017 | $22,459.52 |

**AVERAGE ANNUAL PORTFOLIO RETURNS SINCE START
OF MUTUAL FUND PURCHASES: 10.91%**

The significant difference from the previous example is that over 50% of this portfolio at start was a 6% zero coupon bond, and the remainder is mutual funds buys in 2003 that were maintained to plan ground rules for 14 years. Addition of the mutual funds plan to the safe $9,000 bond at maturity resulted in a $22,459.52 custodial account to help with cost of the grandson's university education. Note that the plan's 10% goal was exceeded in both cases.

A plan application to consider as children or grandchildren come on scene.

# CHAPTER SEVEN

# YTD RETURNS

In Chapter Three, we state the following very important reason for a benchmark:

> At least 50% to 70% of your portfolio must be invested in the best Moderate Balanced fund managers available. To verify that you have **hired** the best Moderate Balanced fund managers, the *average* performance must be known at all times.
>
> If your portfolio YTD return is beating average performance, you will know that your 10% goal will be met or exceeded because of your Category funds, and if not, you will know that you need to take action to improve your returns.

**Here is how you get the current YTD return:**

The YTD is the percent by which the portfolio current value has risen (or dropped) since the January 1 value. To get that number, you must have the January 1 market value, subtract that value from the current value, and divide the answer by the January 1 value.

**Example:** January 1 value was $15,500 and current value is $16,300. When you subtract $15,500 from $16,300, you have a market value increase of $800. Divide that by the January 1 value, and your YTD investment return is 5.61%.

**NOTE:** *If you add funds to your portfolio, the above formula must change to take account of that. In that case, subtract that value and the amount of funds added from the current value, and divide the answer by the January 1 value.*

That calculation was done manually with pen and paper and filed in cabinets for centuries. If you have access to and are comfortable with a computer of any kind, what's known as a spreadsheet has many important advantages.

If you are not familiar with spreadsheets, family members or friends you know can help you learn about how to set up and maintain a spreadsheet. They will not only answer any questions you may have about the specific items in the Index and Glossary lists that follow the Epilogue, but will likely also suggest built-in advantages I've failed to point to in this book.

**Use of a spreadsheet:**
- Will update your YTD instantly when you enter a new market value.
- Is much more easily stored when you save it.
- Is not subject to being mishandled or damaged when retrieved from a file cabinet for updating.
- Can be printed on short notice whenever needed.

# EPILOGUE

*"Do the thing you think you cannot do."*

**—ELEANOR ROOSEVELT**

As this book was nearing completion, the June 23–24, 2018, Saturday/ Sunday edition of the *Wall Street Journal* carried a front page story entitled "Time Bomb Looms for Aging America." The internet version of the headline was a better summary of the ominous point being made: "A Generation of Americans Is Entering Old Age the Least Prepared in Decades." One short paragraph in a long article has specific numbers:

> In total, more than 40% of households headed by people aged 55 through 70 lack sufficient resources to maintain their living standard in retirement, a *Wall Street Journal* analysis concluded. That is around 15 million American households.

So there are many of you nearing or in retirement who fear being financially unready for it, and certainly many more under 55 who know they should be doing more to prepare but don't have any idea about how to begin.

It is my hope that you will have found the answers to the questions in the Introduction to this book reasonable enough to follow up by accepting that YOU CAN *do the thing you think you cannot do*, and begin to explore the specific actions suggested in how-to Chapters One through Four.

As you meet with brokers to evaluate capabilities for providing the information and data mentioned in how-to-buy Chapter Three, you will be with professionals who can answer any questions or suggest research I've overlooked. They'll be patient and pleased to see you more often than once!

The need is certainly very real. It would be very encouraging to get feedback that readers are getting it, finding the plan really does have built-in advantages, and, when acted upon, really does work as well as it has for me.

— Owen Little, June 2018

# INDEX

# ILLUSTRATIONS INDEX

# GLOSSARY

**Allocation:** A synonym for balanced. (*see balanced*)

**Balanced:** Funds that rely on a mix of stocks, bonds, and cash to minimize market risk.

**Benchmark:** A synonym for a returns % standard that must be met or beaten long-term to meet a plan goal.

**ETF:** Professionally managed Exchange Traded Funds consisting of stocks and/or bonds:

- That have defined characteristics, e.g., broad indexes or specific industries, geographic areas, or unique trade philosophies.

- Are traded and transacted during stock market hours.

**Index Fund:** A low management fee portfolio consisting of equities that represent a specific type of fund, e.g., S&P 500, a size of businesses category, or a specific industry.

**Mutual Funds:** Professionally managed funds consisting of stocks and/or bonds

- That have defined characteristics, e.g., broad indexes or specific industries, geographic areas, or unique trade philosophies.

- That are competitively sold to the public during the day and transacted each evening of a trading day.

**No load:** Funds that are commission free.

**YTD:** Year to date.

# APPENDIX

## S&P 500 HISTORY, 1950-2017

| S&P 500 AT END OF YEAR | S&P 500 CAL YR RETURN | DATE | AVERAGE DECADE ANNUAL RETURN | DECADE RETURN |
|---|---|---|---|---|
| 16.66 | | 1/3/1950 | EARLIEST DATE AVAILABLE | |
| 20.43 | 22.6% | 12/31/50 | | 2 minus years |
| 23.77 | 16.3% | 12/31/51 | | 1 less than +3% year |
| 26.57 | 11.8% | 12/31/52 | | |
| 24.81 | -6.6% | 12/31/53 | | |
| 35.98 | 45.0% | 12/31/54 | | |
| 45.48 | 26.4% | 12/31/55 | | |
| 46.67 | 2.6% | 12/31/56 | | |
| 39.99 | -14.3% | 12/31/57 | | |
| 55.21 | 38.1% | 12/31/58 | | |
| 59.89 | 8.5% | 12/31/59 | | |
| | | | 15.04% | 259.48% |

| S&P 500 AT END OF YEAR | S&P 500 CAL YR RETURN | DATE | AVERAGE DECADE ANNUAL RETURN | DECADE RETURN |
|---|---|---|---|---|
| 58.11 | -3.0% | 12/31/60 | | 4 minus years |
| 71.55 | 23.1% | 12/31/61 | | |
| 63.10 | -11.8% | 12/31/62 | | |
| 75.02 | 18.9% | 12/31/63 | | |
| 84.75 | 13.0% | 12/31/64 | | |
| 92.43 | 9.1% | 12/31/65 | | |
| 80.33 | -13.1% | 12/31/66 | | |
| 96.47 | 20.1% | 12/31/67 | | |
| 103.86 | 7.7% | 12/31/68 | | |
| 92.06 | -11.4% | 12/31/69 | | |
| | | | 5.26% | 53.72% |
| 92.15 | 0.1% | 12/31/70 | | 3 minus years |
| 102.09 | 10.8% | 12/31/71 | | 2 less than +2% years |
| 118.05 | 15.6% | 12/31/72 | | |
| 97.55 | -17.4% | 12/31/73 | | |
| 68.56 | -29.7% | 12/31/74 | | |
| 90.19 | 31.5% | 12/31/75 | | |
| 107.46 | 19.1% | 12/31/76 | | |
| 95.10 | -11.5% | 12/31/77 | | |
| 96.11 | 1.1% | 12/31/78 | | |
| 107.94 | 12.3% | 12/31/79 | | |
| | | | 3.20% | 17.25% |

| S&P 500 AT END OF YEAR | S&P 500 CAL YR RETURN | DATE | AVERAGE DECADE ANNUAL RETURN | DECADE RETURN |
|---|---|---|---|---|
| 135.76 | 25.8% | 12/31/80 | | 1 minus year |
| 122.55 | -9.7% | 12/31/81 | | 2 less than +3% years |
| 140.64 | 14.8% | 12/31/82 | | |
| 164.93 | 17.3% | 12/31/83 | | |
| 167.24 | 1.4% | 12/31/84 | | |
| 211.28 | 26.3% | 12/31/85 | | |
| 242.17 | 14.6% | 12/31/86 | | |
| 247.08 | 2.0% | 12/31/87 | | |
| 277.72 | 12.4% | 12/31/88 | | |
| 353.40 | 27.3% | 12/31/89 | | |
| | | | 16.11% | 315.76% |
| 330.22 | -6.6% | 12/31/90 | | 2 minus years |
| 412.73 | 25.0% | 12/31/91 | | |
| 435.71 | 5.6% | 12/31/92 | | |
| 466.45 | 7.1% | 12/31/93 | | |
| 459.27 | -1.5% | 12/31/94 | | |
| 615.93 | 34.1% | 12/31/95 | | |
| 740.74 | 20.3% | 12/31/96 | | |
| 970.43 | 31.0% | 12/31/97 | | |
| 1229.23 | 26.7% | 12/31/98 | | |
| 1469.25 | 19.5% | 12/31/99 | | |
| | | | 16.11% | 315.75% |

**RETURNS: 10.56%** *50- year annual average*

| S&P 500 AT END OF YEAR | S&P 500 CAL YR RETURN | DATE | AVERAGE DECADE ANNUAL RETURN | DECADE RETURN |
|---|---|---|---|---|
| 1320.28 | -10.1% | 12/31/00 | | 4 minus years |
| 1148.08 | -13.0% | 12/31/01 | | 2 less than +4% years |
| 879.82 | -23.4% | 12/31/02 | | |
| 1111.92 | 26.4% | 12/31/03 | | |
| 1211.92 | 9.0% | 12/31/04 | | |
| 1248.29 | 3.0% | 12/31/05 | | |
| 1418.30 | 13.6% | 12/31/06 | | |
| 1468.36 | 3.5% | 12/31/07 | | |
| 903.25 | -38.5% | 12/31/08 | | |
| 1115.10 | 23.5% | 12/31/09 | | |
| | | | -0.61% | -24.10% |
| | | | | |
| 1257.64 | -14.4% | 12/31/10 | | 2 minus years |
| 1257.60 | 0.0% | 12/31/11 | | 1 zero% year |
| 1426.19 | 13.4% | 12/31/12 | | |
| 1848.36 | 29.6% | 12/31/13 | | |
| 2058.90 | 11.4% | 12/31/14 | | |
| 2043.94 | -1.2% | 12/31/15 | | |
| 2238.83 | 9.5% | 12/31/16 | | |
| 2673.61 | 19.4% | 12/31/17 | | |
| | | 12/31/18 | | |
| | | 12/31/19 | | |
| | | | 6.78% | 139.76% |

CPSIA information can be obtained
at www.ICGtesting.com
Printed in the USA
LVHW081243031118
595564LV00005BA/101/P